"This was a real treat, walking so lightly ¿
the profane meet with intelligence, imagination, and lots of charm. I kept
being reminded of Ecclesiastes."

—ALICIA OSTRIKER,
author of *Once More Out of Darkness and Other Poems*

"I'm familiar with many of the things Constam's poems plangently evoke.
. . . Some of the poems remind me, in the best way, of poems by Yehuda
Amichai and Nelly Sachs. . . . From time to time, I also was reminded of
some of the later poems of R. S. Thomas."

—KEVIN JOHN HART,
Anglo-Australian theologian, philosopher, and poet

"I just love these poems! They are such a wonderful deep dive that pulls
me into each experience so evocatively. Overall, what comes through is
the wrestling—wrestling with God, with being faithful or not, with being
secular yet pulled/tied/anchored to this tradition. . . . It resonated with my
understanding of the biblical meaning of 'Israel' as 'he who wrestles with
God.'"

—LEONARD FREEMAN,
author of *Ashes and the Phoenix*

"I enjoyed most the combination of a hard, no-nonsense style . . . with re-
strained lyrical and philosophical flights, passages of insight that are fully
poetic and dramatized."

—A. F. MORITZ,
University of Toronto

"In *Brought Down*, Constam appears as . . . a Seinfeld-mode Job, questioning God about his 'masquerading as the dark.' God is 'arbitrary' and we are fickle; or he is fickle and our intermittent obedience to indecipherably contradictory dicta becomes the real story of each obituary. . . . I thank Simon 'Agonistes' Constam . . . for giving us a newfangled Ecclesiastes. *Brought Down* delivers the goods!"

—GEORGE ELLIOTT CLARKE,
Canadian Parliamentary Poet Laureate, 2016–17

"There is a great deal of self-knowledge in these poems, and it is all slightly painful, a bit absurd, and touched with a humble grandiosity that the poet relishes. He is irrecoverably entangled in Jewishness, and he brings that into the light. For all the suffering and painful contradictions the poems in this book deal with against the historical background of Jewish suffering, the mind that comes through is invariably gentle."

—STANLEY FEFFERMAN,
Atkinson College, York University, retired

BROUGHT DOWN

BROUGHT DOWN

SIMON CONSTAM

RESOURCE *Publications* · Eugene, Oregon

BROUGHT DOWN

Resource Publications
An Imprint of Wipf and Stock Publishers
199 W. 8th Ave., Suite 3
Eugene, OR 97401

www.wipfandstock.com

PAPERBACK ISBN: 978-1-6667-3435-5
HARDCOVER ISBN: 978-1-6667-9011-5
EBOOK ISBN: 978-1-6667-9012-2

JANUARY 7, 2022 10:21 AM

for Janice Waugh and Jacki Levin

Contents

Acknowledgments

I WANT TO EXPRESS my deep appreciation to Mark Kempf, exceptional reader of poetry, for his ongoing comments and criticisms of my work and his endless support of my efforts.

My appreciation also to:

Janice Waugh for her calm and straightforward help with so many aspects of this work including the poems, the structure of the book, and not least her patience while I distanced myself to work on it.

Jacki Levin for unending support and love, and the constant link she provided me to things Jewish.

Tracey Nesbitt for her commonsensical reactions to my work, her proofreading, and her unflagging belief that I have been doing something worthwhile.

Stan White for his willingness to look at and critically consider material far outside his experience.

"Almighty" was first published on the Dark Poets Club, 1/04/2021.

"HaMakom" saw its first publication in the *Jewish Literary Journal* in February 2015.

"Yerushalmi," originally published in *Poetica Magazine,* was chosen as a finalist for the Anna Davidson Rosenberg Award in 2016.

"Judith and Holofernes" originally appeared in *LongCon Mag,* Issue #3, Spring 2020.

"Sarai," then titled Sarah, was published in *Inez Magazine,* August 2018.

ALMIGHTY

You're a Torah scroll.
You're a mountain rock.
You're a page filled with ancient talk.
You're two, brilliant-blue sapphire blocks.

You're a temple wall,
an empty ark.
You're masquerading as the dark.
You're a writer gone mad,
a writer gone to ground,
a writer on the lam.
You don't want to be found.

You're a palimpsest,
an all-too-fallible psychotherapist.
You're a brazen monologist,
a single, lonely, witness to the event.
We won't stop looking for you
wherever you went.

You will be who you will be.
You're a blue screen.
You're the ocean depths.
In the blue of the midday sun,
your throne is all
that's left of you.

See it from here.
You never talk back.
You're a divine hack.
You should be better than that.

1

Every Glory Is Diminished by the Truth

And do I flinch at the mention of Deir Yassin?
And do you flinch at the mention of Ma'alot?

The scroll handed down to me by certain of my historians
now injures me. And the stories your historians told
also misled. They also injure me.

I must not forget your grandfather running from his garden.
And you must forgo your idea of purity.

A great tragedy happened there.
So, there is night,
and it should have made us better.
But it did not.
We are who our ancestors wanted us to be
but that is not enough for us.

Yes, the worst possible dream is that which has us
remember wrongly. Surely, you also have had to forget.
Great tragedies happened there!

But Innocence does not protect me.
And Innocence does not deny you culpability.
And I fear you. And you fear me.

That is why we both have had to leave.
To find a place where our history
was known to almost no one.

TEXT

Rabbi Aharon Zalman Leib brought down
that a wife should be allowed to be present in a room,
unaccompanied, with a man not her husband if
the general society deems the man to be worthy of such trust.
So, doctors she may be with. Lawyers, she may be with.
Policemen investigating a crime, she may be with.
Delivery men, she may not. She must transact the exchange
of money for parcel at her open front door.

The issue of plumbers and repairmen, on the other hand, is a difficult one.
Women should be wary. Passersby may well interpret incorrectly.
This is not to say that exceptions are not possible
for the representatives of well-known companies.
But all agree that cousins, brothers-in-law and
the friends of husbands are not permissible.
So he ruled.

Now it is true that some have disputed Reb Leib's pronouncements.
The philosopher Eliezer Greenshaft, scion of a great rabbinical house,
himself a God-fearing man, looked up into the sky
within which the world floats
and saw as perfectly legible as if on paper God's intention.
Eliezer seated himself at the great oak table his family had owned
for more than 200 years and brought down
onto the page the idea that women should be free
of all rules and restrictions such as Reb Leib had promulgated.

Some say that we do not think our own thoughts, nor dream
our own dreams, that there is a heavenly text
from which we draw the days of our lives. And though
we act upon each other, we cannot be assured
that what we think is causing good
is not rather, deeply wounding.

We know that holiness lies in every place we look.
Therefore, if it is true that our understanding is incomplete
regardless, our behavior never seems to be uncertain.
And if our belief is too unflinching, we may never even need
to understand the world which is.

How hard it is to sit at a desk observing both text and city streets!
Often the two do not reconcile to anyone's satisfaction. Why would God
respect two views inimical toward each other?
And is there anywhere a trial which will settle the matter?
O Holy One, must we resolve ourselves in you?

The distance is too great. And you are so different from us.
We must settle this in ourselves.
Now is when you should stand back,
not allow yourself to be invoked or quoted.

REFUGEE

Her darkness in the darkness
and that she is a nihilist
surprises me.
All refugees think like that, she says,
"Who put you here, who put me there?"

You'd expect her to be grateful
but when she sees that in your face,
she simply asks to whom, for what.
She says all refugees think like that,
"Who put me there, who put you here?"

TELEOLOGY

On the day I stopped wearing *tefillin*,
to mollify my failure, I swore
I would re-join observance
when I turned sixty-five.

But what they had placed upon me,
or I had willingly accepted,
I simply didn't understand. Nor did I grasp
what my actions meant to them
and, therefore, to me.

That I was responsible for holding up the world.
That on my actions rested the possibility of all creation.
That I had taken a shard broken and fallen from the perfection
and placed it back again into the divine and must hold it in place.

My rabbi told me that wearing *tefillin* was just the same as
putting on one's pants.
No thought was especially necessary
or as important as the doing.

This is how it is for Jews.
The doing is the crucial thing.
naaseh v'nishma,
we will do and we will understand.

We will do and then we will study.
We will act and then we will find the deeper meaning in our actions.
We will do the *mitzvot* and then struggle
to find the why and the wherefore.

But on the altar of reason and understanding,
I have also placed my life.

How does one prostrate oneself before the Lord today?
How does one subdue one's being to God?
Perhaps it is symptomatic and also troubling,
the depth of it is almost unbearable,
the enormity of what I will ultimately lose,
is of no help.

Why must I stand before Him?

GOD'S PRAYER

"May it be My will that My mercy will overcome My anger, and may My mercy prevail over My other attributes, and may I conduct Myself toward My children with the attribute of mercy, and may I put them before the letter of the law."

(BERAKHOT 7, TALMUD. RABBI ZUTRA BAR TOVIA SUPPLIES THE TEXT IN THE NAME OF RAV.)

God is a young God, a teenager.
Well-meaning,
occasionally rebellious.
His heart is in the right place.
He thinks He's a lot like you.

God too has an inner voice.
And perhaps He too is unsure of who He truly is.

To us, these stakes are of the highest order
but to God perhaps they are something He can never fully resolve.

After all, for Him the choices to be and become
are innumerable
and meaningless.

Somehow, It Is God Who Prays to Us

He comes when troubles have overwhelmed Him.
He worries what His past has done.
He worries there is no path.
There is no path . . .

He does not use the beauty of His creation to gain our love
though that was all along his plan.

He does not urge us to make things right.
He leaves it to us to see the threads that make a garment whole.

He asks for forgiveness
but this is sticky, isn't it?
How do I forgive for those of us who sit today
enslaved, denied, impoverished, friendless,
for whom the sporadic nature of our God
and also of our help
is permanent?

HEURISTIC

Having constructed out of God the idea of permanence,
but seeing all around us entropy,
we searched until we found the soul
and bound it forever to Heaven.

Unbroken deserts, vast stretches of forest and plain,
water spilling out over the horizon,
we carried these arguments within us.

And laid out time in journals and
bound them to the future and gave them all names
in order to circumscribe each and every single thing.
How else to stop time from its destroying?

But failed and perplexed for what seemed a like purpose
by the endless unseen, we fell to the click and turn
of machinery, detritus that will not disappear,
and our legacy in ruins that outlast us, waste that
we have hidden knowing well enough
that one day it is sure to reappear.

The distance between my birth and my comeuppance
is broad and deep, and widened by love
but still short enough to require a forever . . .
though several molecules this way or that,
a missed step, a missed train, a glance not caught,
a meaning not inferred, a certain failed experiment,
and no such dream would ever have occurred.

THE PLAGUE OF FROGS

*Weissman, Rabbi M. 1980, The Midrash Says: The Book of Sh'mos
Brooklyn. Benei Yakov Publications.*

The version of the Plague of Frogs story in the Midrash as retold in
The Midrash Says: The Book of Sh'mos was the basis for this poem.

From the streams and small still ponds
that decorated the homes of princes came an army of frogs.
And from the Great Mother Nile one hideous supersized frog emerged
and moved down the main dirt road toward the Pharaoh's palace.
And the enormous frog opened its mouth
and vomited a thunderous flood of frogs.
Frogs of all sizes: green, black & green, yellow, and shades
of all the other colors of the universe. And cacophony!
A croaking, shrieking din. And an unbearable, inescapable stench.
Hundreds upon thousands of the frogs leapt
into the homes of the Egyptians and even into Pharaoh's palace,
streaming through its entrances, through the palace hallways,
skittering on the polished floors, leaping into every room,
and even into the Pharaoh's own private chambers
where he lay trying to block out the defiling noise
and struggling to remove the very idea of them
from his eyes, and nostrils, and mouth.
They jumped onto his bed; he could not escape.
They buried themselves beneath the linens, biting him, intruding
even into his body's orifices, even the Pharaoh's body.
And the frogs descended upon every Egyptian house,
and into every open jar, and pot,
and cupboard they went. In every corner of Egypt.

And tunneled into every person's clothing. Not an Egyptian child,
nor was an Egyptian mother spared. Not a room was without them.
And the Egyptians ran out into the streets but even there
they could not escape the frogs. And some Egyptians went mad
and many died until the moment God,
May His name be for a Blessing,
took pity on them
and the frogs withered and shrank and disappeared,
each and every one, until only the stench remained
and Pharaoh lay humbled in his bed.

When morning came, Pharaoh's ministers took their places
at his side to report one piece of happy news.
Through many years a dispute had raged
between Egypt and the people of Kush over a small tract of southern land.
The people of Kush would not relinquish their claim to it.
War had once or twice been waged but no result had been attained.
But now, now the truth was known, the people on the disputed land
had also been deluged by frogs. They, but not those
just to the south of them.
The land, it now could be said with certainty, was Egyptian.

SIMON AGONISTES

I am hiding from Him,
like Adam.
Way down in the labyrinth
of Tokyo's malls,
Eve knows nothing about it,
she thinks it is just a trip,
into the city.

TORSCHLUSSPANIK

The darkening October sky,
the young man milling about with his cultured friends,
torn from his own culture,
separated by just a single doorway.

And then, unexpectedly, a *Baal Teshuva*
on *Kol Nidre*,
Franz Rosenzweig,
Yom Kippur,
1913,
Berlin.

I think of him,
of the music he could not bear resisting
and the world on the other side of the door
that he would not ever be able to ignore.

I wonder if he thought he could pass by this way again,
deciding differently,
or if he could decide
what term of embrace one has to make for any
love to be permanent.
It is only by an act of great will that love can be forgotten anyway.

We stand on the shoulders of indecision.
But I still think of myself as young.
Somewhere, someone will always take me in.
And if I change my mind again,
the armies of the righteous will always be there.
And the *Chevra Kadisha* at the end.
The world has nowhere to go
to avoid confusion.
Every single day a mirror buries the past.
And every single step along the way is full of errors.

HaMakom

We meet in a small place, a shetl shul,
beneath a tallis' embrace. There is a book
in my hands, but I do not need it.
The text is a jail. Behind its black bars
the mind wanders. Behind the music
of the words, the meaning is obscure.
Some say the words themselves are
Prayer. Some say the emptiness behind them
is the God who deigns to meet you there,
dares you, some say, dares
your heart, to be without its meaning,
to come unrooted as a tree would give in
to the wind and a leaf would float to the sea.

YERUSHALMI

Today I seem to have the face of a man I briefly stared at,
on a bus on Rehov King David in the fall of 1969.

I wear the same clothes, dark jacket, dark shirt,
rough tan trousers, dust-scuffed brown boots.

The mirror shows me, grizzled, unkempt,
stocky, stoic, almost seventy.

My face is the face my grandfather wore.
My parents, aunts, and uncles swore the resemblance
is uncanny. My history is clear.

I was one of Titus's captives
marched through Rome in chains.
I collected all my things in a sack
to flee from Ferdinand and Isabella
along the Jew-choked roads.
I missed my fate in Kielce and Bialystock.
I hid in the forests by Kishinev.

I was a soldier in Babel's army caught
in the gaze of my Cossack captor.
Once, I was dazzled by Jabotinsky. I walked
for days to hear him dream. I trusted history.
And then I spent the war in, and somehow outlasted
Bergen Belsen.
I fled to all the countries of the world.
My children are scattered to the far corners of the earth.

And now my son has come to visit me.
He worries that I stay here.
He thinks I ought to live close to him.
But that is impossible.
I am the inheritor of a furious history
that only in this place
can I never
deny or forget.

PHYSIOGNOMY

For Moses to come face to face with Him,
God had to, one world at a time,
reduce Himself through the alternating
darkness and light
of countless existences
while Moses climbed steadily
upwards rehearsing his prayers
dreaming and discarding ideas
not sure whether to pray,
to beg, to cajole,
to complain, or even demand,
to argue, to accuse, to be silent,
prepared to turn back with every step
but he was hopelessly God-addled,
and stilled by Him to a purpose.
God made him holy, separate.
And God made him equal
in all the ways Moses did not want,
or even understand, caged,
lost inside vast blue skies and
grey storms, buffeted by life and death
but even so
face to face with God.
Perhaps he was and perhaps he was not
impressed because they seemed to have been
just two men in an unhappy conversation,
Moses carrying the unwanted others,
wishing it were not so.
And God surprised at how weak
Moses was. Moses surprised
at how unfair and arbitrary God was.

And God finally telling him
they'd get together again soon
one way or another so that
Moses finally turned around and trudged
off to try to tell the others.

FUNERARY BLUES

As idly as she possibly can, she asks
where we'll be buried. She says we ought to,
as a couple, even past the end, stay married.
But her long-dead first husband she already has
placed in primary honor in the family plot.
His name is raised on the gravestone.
What place might I take there and which one not?
Perhaps I ought to be in a nearby grave alone.

Or should I think about Jewish burial somewhere else?
She could remain with her once and greater love as
I am not jealous of a presumed hereafter.
But oh, what will my children, learning this, be thinking of?
And, alas, she and I, on another matter, we're also in disarray
as she favors cremation and I favor decay.

My Own Private Yom Kippur

(I)

From here to the nearest minyan in Seoul,
it is four hours over rough roads.
I go most years in order that I might recite the *Kaddish*
standing at the gates silently among all the others waiting,
diminished by the knowledge that one day
He will not let me pass. I go to be swept upwards
by the cantor's plaint and the shofar's heralding freedom from our sins
and the granting of another year of life.
It is exquisite in the waiting and
exquisite in the painful hope that one might live.

(II)

The intermarried or otherwise inappropriate Jews,
those in same-sex marriages, those with gender challenges,
even those just ordinarily disaffected,
often choose to move from cities to small towns, as if excommunicated.
As difficult as an individual situation might be, so
the further out a person or a family settled.

When my first marriage ended, I sought to be so far away
that I could not easily return. I would be
beyond the reach of any Jews
who might reach out to me.

(III)

Still, once yearly, in as anonymous a way as I could,
I returned to join a *minyan*,
to have a verdict placed upon my head,
to feel myself among my co-religionists.
But I am well-advanced in years now. My need to take my place
within the *Kollel* is not nearly so strong as once it was.
And my wife who knows nothing at all about Judaism understands less
each year about why I need to travel such a great distance
and leave her then behind me.
And so, on this Yom Kippur, to avoid the drowning eddy of a crowd,
to make it easier for my wife who will accompany me,
I will walk out into the cold woods. I will find a small clearing
and from dawn to dusk, in the cold air, I will fast and pray,
and beg God's forgiveness for what I can remember of my sins.
And I will sing the Kaddish—*Yisgadal v'yisgadash sh'mei raba* . . .
and I will apologize for saying it without a *minyan*
so distant from other Jews.
And I will hear the birds' songs as if they are the shofar's blowing.
And I will dare *HaShem* to forgive me.

(IV)

I'm at work. I call my son. I tell him I just want to talk to a Jew
who isn't fasting, isn't praying, has gone equally wrong.
And then for solace I multiply by millions.
But it affords me little comfort.

(V)

Here we are completing every thought God ever had
in physics, biology, chemistry, and poetry.
And trying to sort out all that He confounded us with
in how we love and respect all others.
How is it we still go to Him, atoning for errors made
when His own effort has forever complicated us?

(VI)

The Shabbos before Yom Kippur, I sit in my basement.
I'm irritated that I should be reluctant to turn on the television
or read a magazine. I move to my desk. My desk is an *amud*.
I lean over it and cannot help but imagine myself in shul.
I wonder if God will look and see this and find it acceptable.

(VII)

Carol's out for her morning run. In the best of families, husbands
don't have to tell their wives which days are holy
and which are simply holidays.
But I'm not sure myself how ultimately important this one is.
Perhaps, I'm thinking, God has found His way back to me
like someone at the back door asking for money
or a meal. And I feel I ought to do something for Him.

(VIII)

Several miles from my house, I finally stop the car.
It's a hiking trail. I've been here before.
It's not empty. Several people walk past me. I'm looking
for a quiet place. Soon I find a seat beside a suitable and isolated brook
that runs slowly past my body and my thoughts. And now I want to speak to
Him. And just as I begin, the language of our prayers returns:
the *Sh'ma, Kaddish, Hallel,* the *Amidah.*
Oaths of fealty and praise. But I avoid making vows of any kind.
I pray to be added to the book of life for one more year.
And a door opens and suddenly my voice is fevered.
My soul is subjugated. He has that power over me.

(IX)

I have to battle for my life
as I do on the earthly plane.
The glory of it exalts me
even knowing that one day I will cease doing so.

(X)

The North is making signs that it might attack.
Our home is not far enough from the border to escape.
And no assurance from God will come,
no matter the business of my effort.
Have I already failed?
Regardless, the moments of gratitude we usually reference—
newborns, health, love, and longevity—fill us with tears as much as joy
for what we know will eventually happen. Winter comes soon
to put paid to thoughts of life. And spring is certain to demand
too much happiness.
Consider its yearly silence about its inevitable departure.

(XI)

It is getting close. Speaking to my sister,
wishing her *Gmar Chatima Tova* and a good fast.
And no, I won't be going to shul. But perhaps I'll fast.

No, I won't do that either. I can hear the *Kol Nidrei*
in my head but I don't think it is calling me.
And I think I ought to be able to not participate.

(XII)

It is as if I have to battle for my freedom. As if,
because I don't really do battle.
I am not hearing the voices of my parents.

And my children almost certainly
don't even know that it's Yom Kippur.
I call my daughter, she doesn't know.
I tell her I just wanted to talk
to a Jew who isn't fasting, isn't praying.

JUDITH AND HOLOFERNES

It is not as simple as cutting a man's head off.
You must also sell it to the world
or if not to the world, to literature.

The heroine must be of good character
if not good stock.
And she must save not just herself,
she must save her family, a city, a town,
even if only just a child.
Much is expected of a woman.

And she must be handsome.
Each depiction of her must find her
loathsome
but for her exceeding beauty.

And she must be honored for her difference,
her lack of forebears. And Holofernes's army
ought not to seek revenge
though armies always do.
Such revenge is never spoken of here.
His men scatter out of fear.
They do not tear every hovel and market apart
to find Judith and destroy her town
as surely must have happened in real life.

THE TENTH GENERATION

What can be accomplished in a crowd?
What can be felt in a loud, chaotic place?
There's always the need to break free.

And now you're famous!
Heaven has turned its head toward you.
Now you're tethered to a screen.
It lifts you up, parades you about, exalts you,
and stores the memory of you
in the unlikely event you ever make the news again.

You're back from the dead, is that it?
You surface from the past, you go on living.
But everyone's forgotten you were longlisted, shortlisted, won the prize,
built something to last, cut some serious problem down to size.
The truth is you are being made harmless every day you're alive.

There's no such thing as revolution anymore.
Those who dreamt that up are long gone,
each one of them a *Shabbtai Tzvi*
lounging themselves
in some sultan's luxury.

Nobody can remember anymore
what they filed you under
but a keyword will pull you up.

And down to the tenth generation your children
will stand by ready at a moment's notice to decry
some insignificant slight to your reputation.

18 Benedictions (Lèse majesté)

I used to do this,
take three steps backward
then three forward,
before the King.
I and all the others,
bending like trees in the wind
toward the east.
I used to do this
I did it for years.

But on that day
I took one step closer,
and on the days that followed
two or three,
each step creeping closer
to You being face to face
with me.

See me for who I am,
not a faceless white and black
plan of obedience today I am
going to hold You to account.

You who have everything stand before
me who has nothing.

AMENABLE

I'm amenable to not being governed by my history.
Why test others with what my people have suffered?
I have little patience for those who incessantly remember
their suffering bona fides, hundreds of years of their injurious histories.
Every night there they are scrounging around in the halls of the forgotten.
A young woman told me that the racism her people suffered
will have to be expiated
throughout the entire universe one day.

When I think of my grandmother, once a tempestuous young
communist in the Nalibotskaya Forest,
just now coming to the end of her life
which features blindness and crippling arthritis
in both her hands, I probably shouldn't talk of it.
She confided to me that she murdered several men
and somehow came around finally to almost regretting it.
She had locked it away for so long,
the whole business of fighting back,
she never spoke of it,
even ever to her husband
but she assumed because of my generation
that I'd understand her remorse.

But she also told me that it didn't matter what I thought,
it was finally enough.
Simon Wiesenthal had spent years at it,
but being an old Jew now, she wanted to get past that stuff.
Being an old Nazi is its own revenge, she said.
And for her, why bother now to do anything but live?

You can't murder and expect to be absolved, she told me.
But then she would forget what she told me
and tell it to me all over again.
The tempest of the clock has defeated everything.

She does also occasionally acknowledge
how sometimes it is better to murder than to run.
I guess I'm amenable to that.
I think I understand
that my grandmother was thinking
not just of herself.
I love her so much.

And, I'm amenable now,
if the people themselves were involved,
and to people remembering
even I suppose if it was their grandmother,
or relatives you've never known.
Really anyone, I suppose.
I'm amenable to remembering those who were killed,
those who did wrong,
those who cowered in the face of hatred,
those who fought back,
those who had to do the killing.

ALIYAH

In some religions, you cannot touch the holy books
if several hours before you've had a nocturnal emission
or otherwise spilled your seed,
or even if your thoughts have just visited
prurience, you ought to recuse yourself
from leading a congregation in any sort
of ritual or prayer.

If you think of God as a lover,
some folks do, perhaps we all do,
why He'd prefer chastity to satisfying your libido
I'll never know. In my conception of the great Almighty,
I think He'd take some measure of satisfaction in your
fully satisfied self coming before Him
and not having to always ask for joy.

THE WEIGHT OF A FEATHER

God, I do not want, at sixty-four, to bother again
with the mad cleaning that is required, for *Pesach*:
two floors, four bedrooms, an ancient kitchen, the garage, the basement.
How odd the things that You require . . .

I will no longer search for chometz, pull crumbs
from the corners with a feather and burn them,
sell to the rabbi whatever I cannot find,
pack away all the cutlery and dishes,
cover the tables and the counter tops
and unload again all the *Pesachdik* tableware
I've stored away each year for decades.
I will not host another Seder.
Let all the younger women now do that.
I am done with it.
It is enough.
You can demand no more.
Release me from it.

PESACH

Who today asks down to the last detail,
as the Haggadah exhorts us to,
down to the *revi'it* of wine,
the *kezayit* of matzah,
whether in the absence of children
the *afikoman* ought to be hidden.

And we rush over the business about it being us
in *Mitzraim*. Our people were slaves in Egypt,
isn't that enough, someone always asks.

And someone always says that there are natural explanations
for all the plagues. And someone always mentions the Palestinians.

"Call down thy wrath upon . . . " begins then
and some of us, and always the guests, shift uneasily in our chairs.

And *Eliyahu*, disguised as the cat, no longer comes in
when the door is opened as he used to when I was young.

Saba, it's always a surprise to be so identified,
is a baby boomer who's going to live too long.
Here it is early April and he's already been out on his motorcycle.
To some this is mildly embarrassing.
But he's still needed, the only one with even a smattering of Hebrew,
one of only several now who can remember
how Seders used to be.

Shomeret

As they said I would, I hover close to my body
in a nondescript room in the basement of Benjamin's Funeral Home.
An old woman sits with me.
She is reciting *Tehillim*,
her voice only audible to herself,
speaking on her heart.

Occasionally she looks up.
And now I am surprised to see that I recognize her.
She is the wife of a man I once knew well, David Lipansky,
who passed several years ago from a heart attack.

I am surprised that my perception seems so ordinary,
so earthbound. In the background of myself, I can
feel the brooding emptiness I know is fear.
It is operable, I know that from my studies.
But I cannot yet turn to it.

David wasn't always complimentary to her.
I remember clearly what he told me. That
she always stood in line impatiently
at the butcher, in the bakery.
She couldn't stand the hubbub of a busy place,
the jostling of customers, especially on Fridays
before *Shabbos*.
But I wish now that I had known her.

Now she looks at me. I would prefer she didn't.
She is comfortable with death.
She looks at me calmly.
How often in my life I felt misunderstood.

David told me that he found her
difficult to please and difficult to appreciate.
It seems a good thing to have that view corrected now
though I'm not sure why.

I think that she must be here out of a great sense of purpose.
I can almost read her thoughts. A desire to serve God and humankind
in equal measure in some incorruptible way

She does not eat or drink coffee throughout the long night.
She sits and reads the Psalms peacefully. They seem to soften her.

How odd it is that I can focus on her so easily. I was not
able in my life to love like that, to focus elsewhere beside myself.

How painful it is to say nothing to her,
not to thank her, not to let her see my gratitude.
But I hold on to her presence tightly. I need her to help me
turn only gradually away from all this.

Unexpectedly, I try to think of my daughters.
The ideas I have used to love them are changing.
I am not sure if all of my ideas are not changing.

I remember the German word *umwelt*,
the self-centered world,
what my senses used to teach me.

Only Mrs. Lipansky, Devorah,
remains pillared to who I am,
an old woman wearing black,
I wonder if she even knows I'm here.

SARAI

On her dresser, a messy shuffle of photographs,
some ginger chocolates, a handkerchief,
a vase with dead flowers, a little earthquake of makeup:
lipstick, blush, a calming mask, an empty brush.

On the wall, grandchildren's art and a tiny Union Jack,
and a letter, dated November 1940, that her conversation
often turns to, rebuilding or reviving a memory
she swears she will not lose track of.

She has some harsh words for God.
She's had enough of good behavior.
He's had enough from her.
She won't be burdened any longer
with either His
demands or His favors.
And as I turn
to leave she has this left to say,
"Please tell my daughter
to stop all the silly talk about me
surviving."

CHAZAL

The Talmudic sages sat in darkened rooms and
squalid shetls in the comfort of dispute and prayers
that knit a thousand years of suffering together.

And though the bright green earth,
the babbling blue waters,
and the iridescent sky

astounded them,
these were not enough.
They imagined fountains sprung from rocks,

mountains held aloft,
donkeys speaking,
staffs turned into serpents.

Once in every several years a Jew speaks to them
about things he himself has seen,
oceans without end,

rain that does not stop,
cities of hundreds of thousands
but none of these compelled them
like the scrolled text and the voices
of the Wonder Rabbis and
history, history, history,
made in heaven,
suffered on earth.

MORE LIGHT

This is the wisdom I inferred
from the passing by of God.

Everything is clear. There may be a door.
Death must be a door

and there must be another door.
But if it is your mind, it lies

if it says it is what lies in store
for the devoted, the deeply humble, the learned or the clever.

Study. Study more. Subject yourself
like Timothy Leary, like John Lilly, like Jonas Salk.

Don't study beauty.
Don't be enamored of beauty.

Study what you cannot see.
What you came here for,

a voice said,
speaking to me.

Honored

My mother survived the Holocaust
and was honored for surviving.
She spoke almost weekly
in high school auditoria.

The war is so distant, she told them,
but it is still mine, she said.
I own it by birthright,
she told them.

But she was perplexed by teaching
suffering
and also wanting to forget it,
to chase it far away.

Young men and women understand
that they are being misled
into an idea of courage that is untrue.

She defended her behavior,
she always used to say,
in front of the court of herself
though she knew
her defense did not cohere.

And what's more curious too,
it was in the war she met
my father.
As everyone does, she imagined their love permanent
when she knew that imagining it thus
was the only way
it could be so.

How awful to be wrapped into
a final, hideous quiet of yourself
because you and your lover
cannot pull you completely away
from your savage past.

She would tell me that she wished
that she had done something to deserve
what happened to her. Her victimhood was
a storm of importance
she could never escape.

The world is full of tyrannies,
and wars give all the opportunities
for self-immolation.

She often said she did not want to be honored
and respected for surviving.
There is no wisdom in it.

Someone knows someone, she told me.
She answers the phone. She tells her story.
She tells the truth. She knows where this is leading,
pretending to understand because she has suffered.

WAR STORY

Last night after the poetry reading,
I fell to arguing with the poet.

He claimed he knew no doubt.
The subject was people who come

to take you away in the middle of the night
amid shouts and imprecations.

It reminded me of what my mother said
would be a feature of my life.
That I'd relive the lives of Jews
no matter what barriers I might try to put
between them and myself.

If only they had stood up to their oppressors, he said
to this roomful of unwitting faces
as had his own father who saved himself through
stubborn strength and God's good graces
which honor those, he said, who fight.

There is a God somewhere
and perhaps He is just like he was portrayed last night
and He honors those who fight
and perhaps He is tired of
the never-ending intrusive night
of the weak, and the halt, and the helpless.

BROUGHT DOWN

Blood is a river that will not stop
and its far reaches are fraught with changes
as we are the changes from long ago.

My genes were brought down from Aharon Rabbenu
through countless generations. Not wondering
that his motives may have been impure

in the incident of the Golden Calf. Our quicksilver
intelligence, my father's lineage, my mother's lineage
came down through those long centuries

unscathed somehow by whatever sin or sickness
has befallen all the men and all the women
of all the generations of disaster.

We have suffered. But not me. I have not suffered.
My father, *olav hashalom*, came from a heavenly quietude
that trusted all people.

Too good for this world was what my mother said.
Brought low by this world. Brought down a further peg or two
by me, and later in stories to my children he appeared,

just barely appeared. We can see in each other the men
and women our forebears were—shopkeepers, teachers, musicians,
misnagdim, railway workers, *Chasids*, businessmen.

When I was constituted as a boy, I knew the vast idea of God.
When I fell sick with worry that my father and mother
might die, I knew well enough that God

would do nothing to comfort me. Dwarfed, I spoke harshly to Him.
And He could not defend himself. I think He must have wanted to
but He fell silent, and I spent days and nights pursuing Him

like a lover. I considered Him my equal then, and ever after.
Responsible to me. I brought Him down to stand before me.
What I meant to say is that I brought Him down to stand

with me, beside me. He did so unhappily. It is brought down
that you should not see your father's nakedness
by which we can understand both your father's nakedness

and also the Face of God. You should not see your father's weakness,
your father's dalliances with striving and failing.
It is brought down that you should lift up those parts of the world

which have fallen from divinity and thus make the world
whole again. So should you. So did your fathers and mothers,
for they were brought into worlds of suffering

and we feel that today. Everywhere we look,
there is an explanation of who we are and
who they are and what we might become.
In every room we gather, we see certain things
about ourselves but never speak them.
We see how they have suffered

and humanity suffers, every beautiful child
who came from long, long ago,
down the long river

where hope sang.
Though we ourselves have not suffered.
We ourselves have not suffered.

Glossary

afikoman—A half-piece of matzo which is broken in two during the early stages of the Passover Seder and set aside to be eaten as a dessert after the meal.

Aharon Rabbenu—Literally, our Rabbi Aaron, after Moses' brother.

aliyah—Literally, going up, used both for being called up to the Torah reading and for moving to the Land of Israel.

amud—Lectern, pulpit.

Baal Teshuva—A Jew who returns to religious observance.

Berakhot—Literally, blessings. A tractate of the Babylonian Talmud.

Brought Down—This phrase has several meanings pertinent to this book. The specifically Jewish one means to bring an idea down from the Heavens, or from the Sages; to bring forth into the world; to bring to light, e.g., "Rabbi Nathan brought down the idea . . . "

Chasid—a follower of Chasidism, a stream of ultra-Orthodox Judaism.

Chazal—A Hebrew acronym meaning Sages.

Chevra Kadisha—The Jewish burial society charged with preparing bodies for interment.

chometz—Foods with leavening agents that are forbidden on the Jewish holiday of Pesach.

Deir Yassin—The site of a massacre of Arabs by Jews in 1948.

18 Benedictions—In Hebrew, Shemoneh Esrai, the name of a prayer said daily in religious Jewish synagogue praxis. Amidah or The Standing Prayer, is another word for the same prayer.

Gmar Chatima Tovah—A phrase used to wish someone well for Yom Kippur.

Haggadah—Book that sets forth the order of the Passover Seder.

Hallel—Psalms of praise, 113–118.

HaMakom—One of the names of God. Literally, the place.

HaShem—One of God's names. Literally, The Name.

Jabotinsky—Ze'ev Jabotinsky was a militant Zionist leader in eastern Europe in the early twentieth century.

Kaddish—A prayer of praise to God sanctifying His name. One version is specifically recited by mourners.

kezayit—A volume of food, 1.27 fl. oz., that requires a blessing prior to consumption.

Kol Nidre—Literally, all vows, a prayer recited in the synagogue before the beginning of the evening service on Yom Kippur.

Kollel—A community, study group or institution focusing on the Talmud and rabbinic literature.

Ma'alot—Site of a 1974 Palestinian terrorist attack that resulted in the deaths of 25 hostages.

minyan—A quorum of Jews required to say Kaddish, a prayer in praise of God.

misnagdim—Literally, those who opposed the rise of Chasidism in the eighteenth and nineteenth centuries.

Mitzraim—Egypt.

mitzvot (singular, mitzvah)—Commandments.

More Light—The last words of Johan Wolfgang Goethe.

Nalibotskaya (Naliboki) Forest—In pre-war eastern Poland (present day Belarus), the site of a World War II massacre of Poles by Soviet partisans.

olav hashalom—Literally, peace be upon him.

Pesach—Passover.

pesachdik—Related to the Passover festival.

rehov—The Hebrew word for street.

revi'it—A volume of liquid, 3.8 fl. oz., that requires a blessing prior to consumption.

Saba—Grandfather.

Seder—Ceremonial meal held in the home on Passover.

Shabbos—The Sabbath.

Shabbtai Tzvi—In the mid-seventeenth century, he claimed to be the long-awaited messiah. He eventually converted to Islam.

shemoneh esrai—The name of a prayer said daily in orthodox Jewish praxis. Amidah is another word for the same prayer.

shetls—Small towns where Jews lived in eastern Europe for centuries prior to the Holocaust.

shomeret—A woman who watches over a deceased person from death until burial.

shul—A Yiddish word meaning synagogue.

shofar—An ancient trumpet made of a ram's horn, used for Jewish religious purposes.

Sh'ma—Sh'ma Yisrael is a Hebrew prayer that serves as a centerpiece of the morning and evening Jewish prayer services.

Talmudic—Pertaining to the Talmud which is the accumulated Jewish law and customs found in the Mishnah and the Gemara.

tefillin—Phylacteries which are small leather boxes containing Torah texts on vellum, worn by Jewish men at morning prayer as a reminder to keep the law.

Tehillim—Psalms.

Torah—The first five books of the Old Testament.

torschlusspanik—The anxiety that time is running out and the doors will soon close.

Yerushalmi—In this context, the title is a demonym, what an Israeli would call a person from Jerusalem.

Yisgadal v'yisgadash sh'mei raba—The beginning of the Aramaic prayer called *Kaddish*. These words in English are, "May His great Name grow exalted and sanctified."

Yom Kippur—The Day of Atonement.

Manufactured by Amazon.ca
Bolton, ON

24418962R00035